TABLE OF CONTENTS
DISCLAIMER
DEDICATION
INTRODUCTION
CHAPTER 1. EVOLUTION OF THE RAT RACE
CHAPTER 2. WHAT IS IN A JOB?
CHAPTER 3. WHY DO I HAVE TO WORK WITH THAT TYPE OF BOSS?
CHAPTER 4.
WHY DO I HAVE TO WORK WITH THESE PEOPLE?
CHAPTER 5. BEING IN THE RAT RACE IS A FORM OF MODERN-DAY SLAVERY
CHAPTER 6. ANALYSIS OF THE RAT RACE FROM 3 SOCIAL CLASSES. THE POOR, THE MIDDLE CLASS AND THE RICH.
CHAPTER 7. 9 TO 5 UNTIL 65
CHAPTER 8. PREREQUISITES TO LEAVE THE RAT RACE
CHAPTER 9. WAYS TO ESCAPE THE RAT RACE WITHOUT BEING RICH
CHAPTER 10.
LIFE IS ONLY ONE, MAKE THE BEST OUT OF IT.

Disclaimer

This book was written for entertainment purposes. It is sold with the understanding that the author is not engaged to render any type of psychological legal, accounting, medical or any other kind of professional advice. No warranties or guarantees are expressed or implied. Neither the publisher not the author shall be liable for any physical, psychological, emotional, financial or commercial damages, including but not limited to special incidental consequential or other damages. You are responsible for your own choices, action and results. Enjoy your reading experience.

Dedication

This book is dedicated, to all people that sense that there is something wrong with society's rat race. If you decided to read this book, you have probably sensed that something does not feel right. Perhaps, you have asked yourself: "Is there something else to life other than my daily routine in the rat race?" The answer is yes, there is something else and you are right about sensing that something does not feel right.

"Pay attention to your heart and intuition. They somehow know what you want to become." **Steve Jobs**

Introduction

Have you found yourself starting to feel uncomfortable with your 9-5pm routine? With working 40,50,60 hours or more per week? You are reporting to work every day, yet you are not getting any richer or happier. You feel as if you are in a treadmill to nowhere. Wasting the most productive and energetic years of your life behind a cubicle, a computer or in whatever your job entails. You have probably asked yourself is there something else to life other than this? If you have felt the above feelings, it's obvious that you are sensing that something is wrong. And you know what, your instincts are right. There is something wrong. You are in the rat race. The fate that millions of human beings worldwide must endure for a lifetime.

However, if you are uncomfortable with the rat race, you have an opportunity to get out. Will you have the courage to do it? This book is meant for people who want ideas on how to get out. Hope you make the most of it and enjoy your reading.

Chapter 1. Evolution of the rat race

My definition of the rat race is as follows: You are walking in a treadmill, somebody is holding a bag with money in front of you. To get the money, you need to keep yourself busy running in a treadmill for a predetermined period. It can be a week, two weeks. After completing the time, finally, you get the bag of money. But will you need more money? Of course! So, what do you do? You get back on the treadmill and repeat your cycle. You go to work from 9-5, You go home, eat, bathe, sleep and then the next day, you repeat. You would continue doing this until you are old and can't do it anymore. Sounds exciting right? Wrong, Mankind was not meant to live this way.

I'm not trying to sell you a religion. The following is just for the sake of making an example. I'm sure you have heard of the concept of Adam and Eve. They were in the garden of Eden. They disobeyed. Subsequently, they were cast out of paradise. Their punishment from god, was that they had to work to eat. As a result, many religions nowadays, believe that working was not how humans were meant to live. According to these religions, God's plan for mankind was to enjoy a paradise like lifestyle, Where the land produced fruits without much effort. Working the land is seen as a punishment.

The rat race has existed for thousands of years due to mankind's built-in instinct to survive and increasingly complex lifestyle. Many years ago, during the, cavemen era, the rat race was non-existent.

According to Darwin's theory of evolution Early Humans, were a society of hunter-gatherers. They were more in touch with nature, Using it to their advantage. Cavemen went out each day to hunt their prey. The women foraged for edible plants and brought it to their family daily. They would gather round by the fire and consume the meal for the day. They enjoyed more time of leisure and traveled more than their modern human counterparts. They were nomads who lived a simple life.

Darwin's hierarchy of human needs

As per the theory of evolution the human brain began evolving. Making humans smarter. However, along with the increased level of intelligence, came a more complicated system of life. Today's humans enjoy all the creature comforts that one can imagine. Houses, new cars, yatch, designer clothes, household appliances and the list could go on and on. Unfortunately, these nice things, are the very same things that are contributing to our never-ending relationship with the rat race. People must continue working hard, to be able to finance these prized possession

Mankind has 5 different levels of need.

Need # 1
Consists of the most basic needs. They entail food, shelter, water, warmth clothing. No matter what country you are from, you need these things to survive. As per Maslow, without these basic needs, you cannot continue climbing the hierarchy of needs.

Need # 2
Safety needs, which entail protection of the elements, security, order, law, stability, freedom from fear.

Need # 3
Belonging and love needs, consist of being able to trust and accept others, to be able to receive and give affection and love. Feeling that you belong to a group, (family, church, friends, work)

Need # 4
Self-esteem needs are related to your self-worth. This is when you achieve what you want. They involve mastery, self-reliance, status, prestige, self-respect and respect from others

Need # 5
Self-actualization needs consist of seeking personal growth, self-fulfillment, making your personal potential a reality

In other words, need # 1, takes precedence over the other needs. If you don't satisfy your most basic needs, you cannot move up the ladder and you will not be able to satisfy the other 4 need, which are also very important for optimal human survival. In other words. Having to eat, live somewhere, wearing clothes, water, warmth is a long term and permanent problem, that each human being must find ways to solve. The most common way that most human beings attempt to resolve these problems is by getting a job. And of course, a job will end up placing you in the rat race if you let it.

Chapter 2. What is in a job?

***"If you are doing what mommy and daddy told you to do, go to school, get a job and save money, you are losing."* Robert Kiyosaki**

In this chapter a job will be broken down into different components. I am not trying to demonize jobs. There is nothing wrong with working. However, it is a very important component of the rat race. The purpose of this chapter is to explain why a job is the hardest way of making a living.

Millions of parents throughout the world have told their children: "go to school, so you can get a good job and be a good employee." I was one of those children. To many this is great advice; however, the downside is that this advice sets you up to lose. Why does it set you up to lose? Because you will be always stuck in the rat race.

Many parents basically work only for bread and butter and focus mainly on paying the bills to raise the kids. Their parents, grandparents and great grandparents also did the same. Guess what? This is passed down from generation to generation, and it becomes a vicious cycle. When someone does something different, then the cycle can be broken. I once heard someone say:
"Well we have to be in the rat race. Our parents never left us a large inheritance. The way Rockefeller or Michael Jackson left their kids. That is because this person's parents never did What Rockefeller and Michael Jackson did. They chose to work all their lives for someone else, to pay bills and in doing so, they passed down the rat race

tradition to their kids. This vicious cycle is a major contributing factor of keeping mankind in the rat race.

Jobs resolve your needs for the short run

As I mentioned in the previous chapter. Every human under the sun, has a permanent problem in their hands. They must fulfill their basic needs to survive. Our problems create obligations for us. Most of the population will resort to having a job to resolve their need to survive. Yes, jobs can do the trick. A lot of people feel comfortable and secure when they have a job. However, jobs are a temporary way to satisfy your needs. Why is that you might ask? Well if you think about it all your boss must say are three words to jeopardize your survival. What are these three words? YOU ARE FIRED! Therefore, saying that you are secure in a job is an opinion, being fired is a fact. And then you will be back to square one again. Seeking another temporary solution. Also known as a job.

When you are fired from a job, you have a lot to think about. Such as what will happen to my mortgage, my car payments, the children? Do I have a backup plan such as a savings account? I feel that everyone that has a job needs to have savings in place, which they can use on a rainy day. Jobs are the riskiest way of making your money. I have personally known people who will not buy new house, car, nor designer clothes, due to the insecurity they feel with the job market nowadays. We hear in the news or from family and friends, that companies are increasingly downsizing to save money. Jobs are being cut, companies are closing and so are mom and pop businesses. Employee layoffs have occurred in vast numbers in our society.

The prison without bars

In my point of view, a job is a prison without bars. If you think you are free when you have full-time employment, think again. You share certain similarities to an inmate.
 I am a person who values freedom a lot. I. love my free time so that I can do the things that I want to do. Freedom is golden to me. I have felt trapped, in a full-time job with benefits. Most people would think that a job with benefits is great! To me it's prison.

When you have a job, you are trading your time for money, you don't own your time. The people that own your time, have every right to break your will and make decisions concerning you. They can dictate, when you go to lunch, what time you come in, in the morning, what time you get to go home in the afternoon.

You must ask your superior permission to take a day off, vacation, a sick day. You will be told what to do throughout the day. You only have two choices. You either do as you are told, or you don't do it. If you do the latter of course, you risk being told the 2-letter sentence. You're fired! If you really think about it, is that freedom? Isn't that as if you were in jail? Don't inmates have to go through the same things? The answer is yes. The more you cling to a job and the more you work, the less freedom you will have to do the things that you want to do.
Unfortunately, life is not a bowl of cherries. It's a tradeoff. You must decide what is more suitable to your lifestyle. Do you want to work more, endure more stress and as a result make more money? Or do you want to work less,

make less money, and more free time? Everyone has the solution to this question in their own heads.

Be grateful that you have a job

I interviewed 5 people and asked them about what they hated most about their jobs. The following was what they said. I only included quotations of what they said to protect their privacy. The results were as follows:

Person 1:
"I have to get up at 5 am every morning, shower, help my 4-year-old daughter get dressed. At six, I must travel one hour to get to my mother's house for babysitting. From my mother's house, I must travel another hour to finally get to work."

Person 2:
"I currently live out of my car, because I lost my apartment. I found a job 2 days ago. My morning routine consists of getting up at six in the morning, going to the bathroom at McDonald, bathing with spray bottles, dressing up. Heading to work in my car, looking for parking for 30 minutes, and then finally enter my job."

Person 3:
"My morning commute is horrible, I must get up earlier than I really want. I have to drive for two hours and the traffic can be bumper to bumper sometimes, it can be like sitting in a parking lot. Then I must put up with a boss who is a total jerk."

Person: 4

"What I hate about my job is that I have to deal with people that I don't even like. I have to work with co-workers who will talk behind your back and are hypocrites. You must be so careful with what you say. They can contribute to you getting fired in a jiffy!"

Person: 5

"I haven't had a raise in 3 years. And they didn't consider me for the promotion. Instead, they gave it someone else. All I have been doing, is making the owners rich for the past 3 years. I have thought about getting a different job to get more money."

The testimonies of these five people say a lot. In summarizing their complaints, jobs make you get up earlier than you want to. You must endure all sorts of weather and traffic conditions. Look for parking in cities where it is scarce and risk getting parking tickets. You Do things that you don't really want to. But you do them because you must.

When you have a job, you are obligated to work with people that you don't really like. Plus, with your time, efforts, sweat and hard work, you are making the owners of the company you work for, rich. Often, the employee is not getting compensated as he should. After all the inconveniences that you go through to keep your job, you overhear your co-workers saying, "We should be thankful that we have jobs." Jeez I don't see where that begins to make sense

Jobs can be filled with policies and protocols.

Employees exchange their time for money. This means that an employer can do certain things he wants with you. They are paying you right? This can mean that you must sometimes deal with never ending policies and protocols. Some which might not make any sense to you.

I have worked in jobs where it seems that every week there is a new form to fill out, a new protocol to follow, and in turn this just increases your workload. Some companies act as if they don't know what they are doing. They come up with new policies that do not make sense and they don't care if it makes your work life more difficult. Is as if, they were using the trial and error tactic. If this policy or this protocol does not bring positive results, they change it and come up with a new one next week, or next month or maybe within the next hour? Who knows.

Profits over Quality

"Quality is more important than quantity. One home run is much better than two doubles." **Steve Jobs**

All too often, companies make an indirect emphasis on profits over quality. I have seen supervisors, with a business mayor and no medical experience, making decisions in the nursing department. These executives don't know anything about your profession, yet they affect your day to day work. Usually adding more work or making new protocols that don't make sense, to the people that have to carry them out. As a result, employees will become unhappy and feel overworked and stressed. The quality of their work goes down.

What the high-level executives don't realize is that focusing on quantity can increase profits but in the long run, they will end up making employees unhappy. This in turn, can increase turnover rates and costs of training new staff. Good employees are the leverage companies need to prosper and move upward. So, it is not in their best interest to lose them.

I'm being worked to death

A perfect example of being worked to death is the story that appeared in the news back in 2013. One Ohio man, whose wife died in a car accident sued the hospital she worked in. He claimed she was "worked to death". The lawsuit alleged that from 2011 to the time of her death, his wife's unit at the hospital was regularly understaffed, causing nurses to work through breaks and pick up additional shifts. During his wife's final shift, Beth Jasper, (accident victim), told other nurses she was really stressed and hadn't eaten. That same night she was killed in a car accident. The lawsuit alleged that fatigue from being overworked contributed to the death of the 38-year-old mother of 2.

Often jobs will ask their employees to do mandatory overtime, sometimes, they will ask you to work during days that you plan to take off, or to work weekends. I know of a fellow co-worker that had to quit during her orientation. She learned that, the full-time position she had just started, required a 60-70-hour workweek in an exchange for a set salary. Of course, no additional compensation would be offered for her extra hours of work. She decided then, the job was not for her and she quit

Chapter 3. Why do I have to work with that type of boss?

"Having a bad boss is not your fault. Staying with one is."
Nora Denzel

Types of bosses
As an employee dealing with bosses is an important part of doing your job. As the saying goes 'when the cat is the away the mice will play'. What inspired me to write this chapter was, complaints from co-workers, about bad bosses. They stated this was one of the things, they hated the most about their jobs. I have worked at several different jobs and have come across a variety of bosses, I will mention some of them below:

The I don't have your back boss
In times of trouble this type of boss, lets you sink alone. She will not support you in any way, shape or form. She will bring prove that, she was at a doctor's appointment, when it all happened, so it was not her fault. No blame will stick to her and she will look for an escape goat, if she had to, in order to come out clean.

The You can't please me boss
This kind of boss makes it obvious that she does not like you. She micro-manages everything. All things you do, will never please her. You try your best at everything concerning your job. However, it is never enough. There is always something missing or it's not good. Then you begin to dislike her too.

The I don't know a thing boss

This boss's main characteristic is a pronounced lack of knowledge and incompetence. They always act, as if today is their first day on the job. Employees must explain things to them. Sometimes they make you wonder how they got the job as a boss in the first place!

The vindictive boss

The vindictive boss can be a real sweet heart if you are working at her company. Just don't tell her that you are leaving the company, to work somewhere else. The minute she finds this out, her personality will flip, turning quite unpleasant. After you submit your resignation, she will decide to fire you on the spot!

The manipulator boss

Beware of the manipulator boss. She is self-seeking; A wolf dressed as a sheep. This type of boss has a hidden agenda; to take advantage of you. She will analyze your weaknesses and use them against you. This boss does not listen to your concerns. She will appear helpless without you and use guilt trip tactics to get what she wants from you. Beware, It's only for her own benefit and convenience, not necessarily yours.

Ideally everyone would love to have a wonderful boss. Unfortunately, it's not the case for everyone. Job happiness, sometimes, is not 100%. You could have a great job and a bad boss. It's just part of the work force deal.

Chapter 4.

Why do I have to work with these people?

"Be the attitude you want to be around." **Tim De Tellis**

Part of being in the rat race is having to deal with people that have difficult personalities. When you are working at a job, you are obligated to work with people that you don't like. Below is a list of co-workers, I have had the misfortune of working with:

Types of co-workers

The Tell it all

I remember that at my previous job, one of my co-workers had taken a medication for an allergy. She made the mistake of taking it during the day. As a result, she became drowsy and fell asleep at her desk. Another employee saw her sleeping, called her supervisor and reported her. One hour later the employee who was sleeping, receives a call. It was her supervisor calling to have a talk with her about her sleeping. The tell all co-worker will tell on you before you wink.

The boiling pot

The boiling pot gets really upset when you don't do as she pleases. She will be ready to write you up or set up meetings to have a conversation about something you did wrong. If you accept her meetings, she will corner you and make you feel inadequate.

The traitor

This is the type of co-worker who will pretend to be your friend, and confidant. She will joyfully, go out with you for lunch, talk with you, gain your trust. You will begin opening up to her and when you least expect it, she will stab you in the back, telling people juicy details about your life.

The slacker
This type of co-worker plays dumb so that she will not have to carry the load. If you have the misfortune of having her in your team, she will delegate a lot of the work to you. In the meantime, she will do the least amount and slack off.

The clique employees

These types of co-workers like to form groups of friends. Once they have their clique established, they will alienate you. You will never feel as if you belong in their group. Often, you will end up sitting alone at lunch time.

Having to deal with all these different personalities, can be a turn off. It can make working at one's job more unpleasant. I know it was a turn off for me and made me want to step out of the rat race a lot sooner.

Chapter 5. Being in the Rat race is a form of modern-day slavery

"Slavery and freedom cannot exist together." **Ernestine Rose**

Being in the rat race is very similar to the days of slavery. While many people may argue that slavery is over, it is not. If we look at history. In the year 1850, a guide was written for slave owners. It included 5 different slave rules which helped masters have a better handle over their slaves. After reading the five rules, I saw some similarities between today's workforce and the 5 rules for slave owners. Below, I will be discussing, how the two are similar.

The 1850 publication for slave owners

The five 5 rules

Slave rule #1
Maintain a strict discipline and unconditional submission
We can see this first rule manifested in today's work force. Employees cannot do whatever they want. Companies have rules, policies, protocols. If you peek at an employee manual, you will be able to see codes of conduct, dress codes, ethical matters, chain of command procedures, behaviors that can get you fired, and the list can go on. There are also deadlines that you must adhere to. A company can tell you that a project is due in 24 o48 hours or whatever the need may be. Employer rules must be obeyed. Otherwise you will face consequences. Perhaps being called into the boss's office to be spoken to, being written up, Worst case scenario, you're fired!

Not only are employees required to obey rules, they are also required to maintain a level of submission. You must do your work, be a good pet. Every time you want a day off, vacation, you must run it by your boss who will either approve or decline it. You must go to lunch and breaks when they say so. Your will is broken

Slave rule # 2

Improving living condition of one's slaves in order to induce them not to run away.

During the era of slavery, the slave owners provided shelter, food and some form of medical attention to their slaves. In today's workforce, employees are provided with a salary, so that they can pay their rent and eat. They might be offered health benefits at cost. Some employers even try to provide their employees a decent salary so that they don't run away from the company.

Slave #3

Create a sense of personal inferiority so that "they know their place".

In a job that I had at one time, I heard one of my co-workers say the following: "I will get back to you on that one, I have to speak to my superior first." So, if someone is your superior, what does that make you? Obviously their inferior. Employees can't go around changing policies or making decisions about a company. To do that, is not within their scope. They must 'know their place' and consult with their bosses first to avoid conflicts.

Slave rule #4

Instill fear

In the past, fear was instilled in the slaves. The slaves that behaved badly were made into examples. They had to endure physical and emotional torture. There were slaves who didn't dare to do what they really wanted to do out of fear of being sold, beaten or even killed. As an employee your biggest fear is the fear of being fired. Guidelines are given to you to read, which inform you of activities that can get you fired. The boss might say it himself verbally to you.

Slave rule # 5

Deprive access to education and recreation to ensure that slaves remain uneducated, helpless and dependent.

The business owner you work for, is not going to teach you all their secrets or tricks of the trade. If they taught their employees all their secrets. They might be put out of business by their own employees. Government also tend to keep people uneducated. They don't teach kids much about financial education that can make them rich. This lack of knowledge keeps people uneducated, helpless and dependent, and of course, this ignorance will make someone else rich.

If you like the role of employee, the following applies

"Choose a job you love, and you will never have to work a day in your life." **Confucius**

Some people get angry when you mention the disadvantages of being an employee. They defend that having a job with fringes is great. It's not their fault that they think this way. It is society that has ingrained this notion in our psyche.

Society feels that, the best way to make our money is by going to college, getting a good job and work until you retire at the age of 62, 65, or even70! And if you want even more money, you get a master's degree or better yet a PhD. Sad truth is, these high-end degrees will not take you away from the rat race. If anything, you might have to cling more to it.

From a very early age, students are asked:" *what do you want to be when you grow up?" I want to be a fireman, a pilot, a doctor, and so on."* Is what they say. It would be very rare to hear a student saying: *"I want to own a very large corporation and employ lots of people"* or "I *want to own apartment buildings and rent them out."* The answers are mostly related, to wanting to work for someone else. In other words, be an employee.

There is nothing wrong with liking jobs or working. However, it is the hardest way to make money, but it is acceptable and honest. If you like being an employee go ahead. However; you need to sit down, and ask yourself: is this the job that I really want to do? Don't just do a job for the money, or for any reason other than, it is really what you like to do. You need to make yourself happy first. If you don't like your job, you will not reach your maximum potential in it. It will just become a way of putting food in the table and paying your bills. This does not sound like an interesting way to live.

Chapter 6. Analysis of the rat race from 3 social classes. The Poor, The Middle class and the rich.

The poor and the rat race

"Surround yourself with only people that are going to lift you higher." **Oprah Winfrey**

I have been poor and had family and friends who were also poor. I was able to see growing up, that poor people's focus is surviving. Some mainly work to satisfy their most basic of needs. Many times, they are not able to adequately support themselves and often struggle financially. Many poor people request government help to help pay for rent, food, and other necessities.

Many can be reluctant to create opportunities or ventures for themselves and will have excuses that prevent them from focusing on their success. They succumb to fear and are not risk takers. Also, they often seek the security of a 9-5 job. and prefer to work hard and trade their time for money. Most will not seek the advice of people that could lift them or inspire them to improve their situation.

Most find it difficult to save. They will spend their money on their bills and on things, and live paycheck to paycheck.

I knew one poor person who filled 4 sheds with knickknacks that she had collected over the years. Those things, she didn't really need or used.
I have visited apartments of people who hoard things, that they ordered from QVC or bought at Walmart or thrift shops. Their apt is filled almost up to the ceiling with

things. These very same people continue to struggle financially and are always in debt. They will always have a need to work for someone else.

In summary unless the poor change their way of thinking, they will always be in the rat race, and will have to work until their retirement years. Getting out of the rat race would only be a very distant figment of their imagination.

The middle class and the rat race

"Keeping up with the Joneses impresses the eyes of others and breaks the bank of brothers." **Indiana Quezada**

Throughout my adult life I have mingled with middle class people and observed their patterns. Here is what I have noticed about them.

It is important for middle class people to keep up with the Joneses. If the Joneses have a big house, they also buy a big house. They like brand new cars, some are always buying the latest gadgets. Namely, expensive smartphones, tablets etc. They are into name brand clothes, and not to mention designer accessories. Some want to appear rich by owning all these possessions, but their idea of being rich is a far cry from reality.

The middle class are into going to college, getting a good job, with a great benefits package. Their recommendations to get more money is as follows:

1. climb the career ladder
2. get a raise from the boss
3. get a promotion
4. Work overtime

5. get a higher degree such as a masters, or a PhD.
Sure, these things can help get more money. But what is the catch? Most often than not, as the middle class make more money, they also end up spending more money on high priced consumer goods. Perhaps a higher mortgage due to a bigger home and an increase in real estate taxes.

The Middle class may feel a strong urge to upgrade. They might start living in an apartment. From an apartment, they upgrade to a small house. From this small house they will upgrade to a bigger house, and so their expenses will continue to rise. Some middle-class people get uncomfortable when they visit the house of a frugal person. They just can't imagine living in a frugal way! Let alone downsizing and letting go of all creature comforts at their avail. What the middle class don't understand is that owning all these things, comes with a cost. What is the cost? Always being in debt, paying expensive bills and being owned by their possessions. What the latter means, is that when material things, keep you working hard to pay them off. They really own you. You don't own them. Sad but true.

The retirement plan of the middle class might look as follows:
1. 401k account
2. Working until retirement age 62,67,70 and let the government take care of us.
3. Never retiring and working until death

Unfortunately, the above retirement plans will keep you in the rat race your entire life. The middle class usually make salaries that by American standards are decent. They have the ability of leaving the rat race if they change their way of thinking. This group does not have much

freedom to leave. They are busy being slaves to their debt and lifestyle.
How the Rich see the rat race

"The rich don't work for money, but money work for them." **Robert Kiyosaki**

I admire rich people. What I admire about them, is their intelligence when it comes to creating wealth and empires. They see money were others don't see it. They have vision. In other words, they see money with their minds. They take risks and don't let fear stop them.
Rich people don't work for money. They value their freedom. And would feel trapped in a rat race situation. Instead, rich people make their money work hard for them. They understand that money works harder than oxen and beasts of burden when you put it to work, and as a result, you won't have to work for money.

They create abundance for their family and do not focus on lack. I love the fact that the rich can do the things that they want to do when they want to. They don't have to ask a boss permission to take a vacation or keep wondering where their next rent payment and meal will come from. They can decide to take a cruise to Europe whenever they want. They have the freedom to do this. I think it is a great life that many humans on earth wish they had.

Rich people sense that the rat race is wrong. But instead of complaining or day dreaming about getting out, they do something about it. They decide not to do what most people do. Get a job, work hard until retirement. This does not make any sense to a rich person.

I was looking at a YouTube video made by self-made millionaires and YouTube stars Kong and Jesse. Kong was explaining that when they first started out, they wrote in a, notebook several business ideas. They tried every one of those ideas and each failed. After many tries, they came up with a new idea and finally succeeded. Subsequently, they went on to become millionaires.

That attitude shows that the rich understand that failing is part of succeeding. They don't focus on their failures. Rather they move on and devise a plan on how to do it better next time. They enjoy the benefits of being wealthy and are committed to stay that way, and I couldn't agree more.

Chapter 7. 9 to 5 until 65

Why the 9-5 until 65 rule is wrong

Most people have a similar mentality. Go to school, get a good job, save money if you can. Work until you are 62, 65, or 70 which ever age you feel like retiring and retire. When you retire, uncle Sam will take care of you.

Uncle Sam knows what he is doing better than most. The older that you choose to retire, the more money the government will give. This concept works in uncle Sam's favor. Many times, people don't live for too long after they turn 70. You will get more money if you retire younger. Uncle Sam has figured out that you probably will live longer if you retire younger and thus, they will pay you less. According to social security trustee report, social security could run out by the year 2034. Many people could end up without that safety net that they have worked all their lives to get.

People will work for 40,50 plus years and will retire at retirement age, to enjoy only 10-20 golden years if not less. This math does not sound right. To me it sounds better the other way around. Work 10-20 years and even less to enjoy 40-50 plus years in retirement.

What pension plans can do to you

When it comes to pensions. They are not what they used to be. As companies go broke, pensions are rapidly disappearing. I knew a lady who is 64 years old. She said that at her job, she was offered a pension, if she would put in the time. She put in the time which was 20 years to be exact, and when she was ready to collect her pension; she was offered a whopping $20.50. She asked the company on more than one occasion if this was correct. "yes": they responded," twenty dollars and fifty cents it is." I was in disbelief when I heard this. You put in all those years of your life to make someone rich and at the end you get that? It sounds like working for peanuts.

Why it is a good idea to retire from the rat race early

As we know our bodies deteriorate with time. Humans are like cars. As you age, you could need repair or replacement of certain parts. The following will depict brief descriptions of the changes that the human body undergoes with time.

Early adulthood ages 20-40
This is the time that the human body is at its peak in terms of cardiac functioning, muscle strength, reaction time and sensory abilities.

Middle adulthood ages 40-60
At this age your physical strength and functioning begin to decline. Hair can begin to thin and turn grey. You may begin noticing health conditions setting in.

Late adulthood starts at age 60-lasts until death
Physical functioning and stamina are significantly reduced. Chronic and debilitating illnesses can surface. Increased susceptibility to psychological and mental disorder.

Despite the notable physical deterioration that may occurs in one's 60's, most people are aiming to retire in the late adulthood stage. Some want to work until they can no more.

This does not make any sense. Why would you make plans to travel and do the things you want to do, at an age where you might develop, debilitating diseases, which could affect negatively your quality of life. How do you know, you are going to be alive in your sixties? There is an adage that says:' Death and taxes are the only things that are guaranteed in life' and there is a lot of truth to that.

So, when is the best time to make efforts to get out of the rat race? The best time to start is now! The younger you do it, the better. Your body will be in better shape to enjoy, the great things that life has to offer. Plus, you will be able to enjoy yourself for more years.

Chapter 8. Prerequisites to leave the rat race

Change the way that you think

"The greatest discovery of all time is that we can change our future by merely changing our attitude." **Oprah Winfrey**

One of the biggest changes that you need to make is, you need to change the way that you think. You need to understand that leaving our comfort zone is often accompanied with risks and involves overcoming your fears and saying yes to adventure. There are certain words that you must change in your vocabulary. Namely, instead of saying: "It's not possible." it is better to say "I will analyze the possibilities. "when you say the latter, you allow your brain to look for possibilities to make what you want, come true. Sometimes it's not a bad idea to believe in the Nike slogan:' Just do it.' Of course, you must make a calculated decision and analyze if something is for you or not. If you can't say yes to or eliminate the following words, you will have to accept and come to terms with the fact that the rat race will be your fate.

To get out of the 9-5 rat race rut you must say yes, to the following:

1. Risk

2. Aventure

3. Simplicity

4. Change

Eliminate these sentences from your vocabulary:

1. I can't do it

2. It's not possible

3. I will fail

Instead tell yourself:

1. I will analyze the possibilities

2. I will succeed

3. It's possible

Life is a tradeoff

Leaving the rat race is a trade off

"Life is a trade-off. Sometimes you have to get out of your comfort zone, in order to gain what your heart truly desires." **Indiana Quezada**

Leaving the rat race is a tradeoff. I take it that since you are reading this book you are already interested in doing something besides the rat race. That makes you a step closer to accomplishing your goal. Before I show you the different paths you can take to move yourself away from the rat race. I must tell you that moving away from the rat race and living life on your own terms comes with sacrifice If you are not willing to make changes and step out of your comfort zone, you cannot have any aspirations to step out of the rat race. When you look for too much security and safety nets in your life, it comes at the expense of your freedom and happiness. It does not make sense to embrace boredom, bad jobs and drudgery in your life.

Be frugal and adopt a simpler way of life

Frugality and savings are two arrows that point in the direction of freedom. **Indiana Quezada**

To some people the concept of being frugal is crazy. They can't fathom the idea of downsizing, living on less money. They don't know how to be frugal. Some people even get angry if you suggest being frugal.

If you want to leave the rat race, you must cut down your expenses. In other words, down size your lifestyle and adopt a life of more simplicity.

You also need to stop thinking that:

1.) Keeping up with the joneses is a good idea.
2.) He with the most toys wins.
3.) It's impossible to downsize your lifestyle.
4.) A life of frugality and minimalism is not for you.
5.) Maxing out Credit cards is a good idea

Be wise when choosing your bills

"The power to choose you financial predicament and how hard you are going to work, is in your hands." **Indiana Quezada**

Before starting a family, you decide how many kids, you are going to have. The more kids you have the more it will cost you. Kids are expensive. You can decide if you are going to live in a 700 square foot apt or a 3500 square foot house. Whether you are going to drive a Mercedes Benz or a $ 5000 used car. Lastly, whether you are going to buy designer clothes or simpler ones from the thrift store. The power to choose your financial predicament and how hard you are going to work is in your hands.

Life can be a tradeoff. In order to gain something, you must lose something. If you want to get out of the rat race you must make certain sacrifices. If you don't want to make any sacrifices and step out of your comfort zone, you cannot have any aspiration to have more free time or get out of the rat race. When you look for too much security and safety nets in your life, it comes at the expense of your freedom and happiness. It extends drudgery in your life.

Our ancestors led simpler lives than we do today. They survived without all the creature comforts that we are used to today. The truth is, humans do not need so much to live. It is consumerism and the capitalist business world that has led us to believe that we need a lot of stuff. I get circulars all of the time advertising sales, 80% off this item, buy one get one free or get 50% off. Act fast, act now, last act! are all sales pitch that stores use to get you to buy things. You must have will power and not succumb to these temptations.

Some examples of adopting a simpler life are:

"Material things are obstacles that bar you from being free to do what you really want to do." **Indiana Quezada**

If having a full-time job with benefits, the big house full of furnishings, a brand-new car, designer clothes, shoes and accessories etc. sound appealing to you, you can continue this lifestyle, it's your choice. However, you are not going to have much freedom. You will be a slave to your debts. Namely, 30-year mortgages, property taxes, car notes, maintenance and repairs, credit card debts and the list can go on. Material things will rule your life. They are obstacles that bar humanity from being free to do what you really want to do.

Downsizing your abode

Do you really need to live in a 2000 square foot home? Have you thought of renting a smaller apartment that meets your needs and costs less? In the long run you will be saving a lot more money. If you live in an expensive city, you might want to move to a cheaper state where the rent is less.

Food shopping

When food shopping, Look for coupons. compare which supermarket has the best sales and shop there. Before food shopping, check your fridge first, to avoid buying things double. Don't buy more than what you need because an item is on sale. If your food spoils and you must throw It out. It is not much of a savings.

Car options

If you are thinking of buying a brand-new car think again. You are going to have car payments plus your insurance will be more expensive. I once bought a car in decent condition for less than $5000. It took me from point A to point B with no problems. Of course, I had a mechanic take a look at, so that I wouldn't take home a lemon. The car was good, and I had no car notes to pay and couldn't be happier.

Clothing and accessories

Before buying anything new. Check out the thrift stores. Stores like goodwill and savers, can carry great deals on quality, second hand clothes, shoes and accessories at a fraction of the cost of getting designer items.

In summary, adopting a frugal lifestyle and injecting your life with more simplicity, will help speed up your exit out of the rat race. However, you must be disciplined enough to stay committed to this lifestyle.

Credit card debt

It is better not to have credit card debt. The best thing is to Save money and pay for what you want in cash. Your item will be completely paid for and you will not have a bill at the end of the month. When you keep a credit card debt, interest continues to accrue on your original purchase amount and you end up paying way more than you expected.

Chapter 9. Benefits of leaving the rat race

"Escape the rat race and get into the horse race (your own dream)- that is the real deal." **Bernard Kelvin Clive**

Reduction of stress related illnesses

I remember one time when I used to work in the jail system. My job was that of an auditor. I was supposed to audit the charts of the inmates and abide by all regulations and deadlines. As an auditor, I was not the favorite employee. It was my job to scrutinize the clinical staff's incomplete work and bring it to the attention of their superiors at the end of the week. They were not pleased, when their supervisors brought to their attention their dirty laundry. I would experience animosity and at times, I would be shunned by the staff. I recall being under a lot of stress at that time. I used to take my job very seriously maybe a little too much. I hardly took days off.

Overtime, I felt the work stress piling up, to the point that my mind started to play tricks on me. I started to feel palpitations, cold hands, increase in blood pressure and light headed. Ultimately, I ended up having a nervous breakdown and had to be escorted out of the facility by emergency personnel.

As I took a few days off and eventually changed jobs, I started to feel better. I'm a firm believer that job stress has a direct negative impact on one's health. According to Doctor Michael Miller from the university of Maryland school of medicine, 'workplace stress is bad for your heart.' Heart disease is one of the top killer of Americans.

In conclusion an early retirement can be beneficial to one's health at it decreases the chances of serious illness.

More time with family

This one is self-explanatory. When you leave the rat race, you will have more time for your family. Throughout my lifetime, I have heard on more than one occasion wives complaining to their husbands about how he works too much and does not make time for the kids. The husbands go on to say: *"Well honey, I have to pay the mortgage, the bills and give the kids the things that they want."*
"I know, but the kids don't have your presence, which is so important to them." The wife responded.

It is in human nature to want to spend more time with family. However, with the demands of certain jobs it's difficult to spend the time you want with your family. When you become free of the rat race you will be able to dedicate more time to your family and do the things you love to do with them.

More time to work on your dreams

"The problem with having a job is that it gets in the way of getting rich". Robert Kiyosaki

According to Robert Kiyosaki, a job gets in the way of working on your dreams. When you exchange your time for money, you are working hard to accomplish someone else's dream and not your own.

You may have to, get up early every day, work long hours and do overtime to meet your job's demand. At the end of those long hours of work, you come home tired. You might just want to rest for a while and you still must prepare to go to work tomorrow. What time will you have to work on your dreams? The answer probably very little.

More time to live life and what it means

To me, the things that bring the most happiness are those things that cost nothing. Some examples are: A beautiful mountain view in the country, being surrounded by good friends and family and the list can go on. There is an obvious difference between living life and just existing. Humans should live life not exist in life. Living life means engaging in activities that bring you pleasure in a good-natured way. Below are examples of living and existing in life:

Living life
1. Visiting a country that you always dreamed of
2. Spending more quality time with loved ones
3. Being your own boss.
4. Living life on your own terms not someone else's
5. Sitting relaxed in front of a beach enjoying the ocean view. Perhaps sipping your favorite drink.
6. Surrounding yourself with positive people
7. Achieving your most coveted goals.

Existing in life
1. Reporting to a job that you hate, but you do it because you must pay the bills
2. Having conflicts due to not spending enough time with loved ones
3. Being dissatisfied and bored with your life.
4. Being in the rat race for the long haul
5 Maxed out credit cards waiting to be paid

After reading the above lists, you should have an idea which list made you feel sunny inside and which list made you feel drained and uncomfortable. I can tell you that just imagining doing the things under the list of living life categories, made me feel good. On the other hand, the list of existing in life, made me feel taxed, and heavily burdened.

Life is only one and I want to make it as good for myself as possible. I feel that one should at all cost avoid just existing in life. Instead one, should try to live more. I have accomplished being able to live more and stop existing by doing the things below:

1. Letting go of things that make me feel burdened.
2. Finding ways to embrace things that I find enjoyable

Chapter 9. Ways to escape the rat race without being rich

"Follow your own passion not your parents', not your teachers'...yours." Robert Ballard

Turn your passion/hobby into profits

Analyze what your passion in life is. Working in your passion will not feel like work. It will be an enjoyment for you and that increases the happiness in one's life. You will also be more in touch with your purpose in life.

Your passion could be your hobby. It's not a bad idea to turn your hobby into a business. Below I will give you tips on how to turn your passion in to an income producing venture:

1.Become an expert

Once you realize what your true passion is become an expert in that field. If you lack knowledge. Do your research. Go to the library or online. Take classes about the topic, in order to gain more knowledge and expertise.

2.Have a business plan

Before opening any business. It's paramount that you have a business plan. It is a guide of the strategies that you will use to start, operate and maintain your business. You can read the article in the link below. It talks about how to make a business plan step by step:
https://www.Entrepreneur.com/article/247574/business plans: a-step-by-step-guide

3.Find ways you can make money with your passion

Think of the different ways that you can make money. Perhaps teaching other people about it, sell products, open a store, starting a blog.

You can create your own website where you can blog about your passion. When blogging it's important to update your website with your articles, regularly and write to your audience as if having a conversation with them. In that same blog, you can sell your services or products. Below are links of companies that allow you to make your own website:

http://www.godaddy.com
http://www.wix.com

Opening your own online store

Nowadays, you don't need to rent a storefront. Well, you can if you want to. However, With the internet, your next store could be several clicks away. Selling your arts, crafts or products online is a possibility thanks to websites such as Wish, Amazon, Shopify. These websites have made it quite convenient. Below, I am sharing links that will allow to research the possibilities of opening you own online store:

https://services.amazon.com/content//sell-on-amazon.html

https://merchant.wish.com/

https://www.shopify.com/tour

Escaping the rat race through real state.

"If you don't find a way to make money while your sleep, you will work until you die." **Warren Buffet**

Using the equity in your home to your advantage

If you have owned a home for a while, and you have equity. It could be your ticket out of the rat race. If for example, you bought your house for 100,000, and its value has increased to 350,000, you now have 250,000 in equity. With these 250,000 dollars, it could be possible to buy several apartments or even 2 houses or more. If in your state, properties are too expensive, you can buy in a different state or even in a different country where real state is even more economic.

There are states where you can buy a house for less than 100,000 dollars. If you decided to buy several homes with your equity money, you can live in one of the properties and rent the others. The rent you collect can provide passive income to finance your cost of living and you will not have to work as hard. You would be making money in your sleep.

If you don't want to deal with tenants, you can always find a property manager in your state that will do the dirty work for you, for a fee. The key is that you need to invest your money on income producing assets. The higher the equity in your home, the more you can invest, and the more you can earn.

However, before you engage in any real estate investment venture, do your homework, so that you know what you are getting into. Check out the neighborhoods, hire property inspectors that will tell you if the property is a total flop. You need to safeguard your money from loss. Find out what the taxes are like, what the market rent is, get a feel of how much cash can flow into your pocket with the properties you purchase.

Renting property that you own

If you don't want to sell your home, you can rent it, and move into a simpler apartment. If when renting the new apartment, (where you will live), you find that rent is too expensive, consider a less expensive state. The rent you collect from your rented home, will help pay the rent in your new apartment and depending on the rental income, you could live rent free. Living rent free, eliminates a person's biggest expense, rent or mortgage. You will have to work less if you have no rent or mortgage to pay.

If you own commercial property and the type of business you are conducting in it, is not your passion or you want to retire earlier to do something different, you can consider renting out this commercial real estate. In some cities, commercial real estate rent for a very handsome sum of money.

Converting your property into a multi-property home

In America, it is very common for people to increase the square footage of their homes by adding additional living spaces. Doing this, will give you a larger home. However, you will not have any cash flowing into your pocket from this larger house. Instead, if you were to convert your one family home into a multi-family property, you could see profits coming your way. I converted a one family home into 2 independent apartments. Both rented quickly, and I ended up with 2 additional sources of income. I have seen property owners who converted their home into 2 and 3 independent apartments, on top of that they turned the basement into an apartment too and also rented it out. Thus, increasing even more their cashflow. Of course, you need to find out if it is legal in your state to rent out the basement. Also, before you convert your home, you need to contact your state's municipality and learn the laws and building codes, for your particular state. It is wise to abide by state laws to avoid future problems. From experience I can tell you that converting a home into a multi-family one can increase your earning potential significantly.

Converting your property into a mixed-use property

A mix-use property is one that is used for different purposes. For example: A property where the first floor is converted into a commercial space and the second floor is a 3-bedroom apartment. The income you can receive from a mixed-use property can be higher. You can charge more rent for commercial real estate. However, keep in mind that due to zoning laws, conversion into a mixed-use property in some neighborhoods, is illegal. Some areas are strictly residential. Before you do this, you need to contact your county office to find out what the zoning laws for your neighborhood.

In conclusion real estate investing is a great way to escape the rat race. For me it was the best way to scape. It provides passive income. It is a way to put your money to work for you so that you don't have to.

Hosting short-term vacation rentals

The founders of short-term rental platforms, namely, VRBO, AIRBNB, saw that there was a market for this way ahead of anyone else. They had a vision. These platforms allow you to rent your entire home or part of it, to tourists and get paid for it.

You prepare your home so that it can be tourist friendly and you set your nightly rate. You can rent a single room, several rooms, or even your entire home to tourists, who often stay on a short-term basis. You can do this part-time or go full time as you wish. I think this is a great business. It can be quite profitable. If you are successful at it. It could provide passive cashflow that can be higher than renting to a tenant. To learn more about short term rentals. You can visit the following links:

https://www.airbnb.com
https://www.vrbo.com

It's important that you investigate tax responsibilities and find out if the short-term rental business is legal in your state. This type of business has been banned in some states. I remember reading an article of a woman who was fined 10,000 dollars for conducting Airbnb business in her NYC apt. However, if it is illegal in your state, don't let that discourage you. Perhaps it's not illegal in your neighboring states. Lastly, you don't have to limit yourself to doing short-term rentals in your home country. You can explore the possibility of doing this business in other countries as well.

The Job vs Freedom ratio concept (JFR)

The Job vs. Freedom ratio is a concept that I developed to help me achieve my freedom. It is an idea that I religiously applied in my life to stay away from drudgery. It spared me from having to work all year in a job. It is about gradually weaning oneself from the rat race. However, one has to be committed to the concept in order to do so.

I worked at a job certain number of months during the year. The months that I wasn't working at a job, I worked on making my passion come true. The funds that I made from both, working at a job and from one of my passions, which is real estate, I invested it into more investment properties. I did this repeatedly, until I eliminated the rat race completely. Before practicing this concept however, I made sure to reduce my cost of living to the bare minimum. This is because slavery and freedom cannot exist at the same time.

Everyone is different and should establish a ratio that is convenient, depending on one's financial situation. Realistically, speaking Escaping the rat race, can be done gradually as opposed to cold turkey. I established my own Job vs freedom ratio (JFR). It became like this:

First year JFR ratio 6:6

Work at a job---------→ for 6 months

Freedom to work on
My dreams----------→ 6 months

Invest income from job and

Working on my dreams---------→ into my passion

For several years I continued to invest the money I made at my job into my real estate investment and my ratio dropped even more. It is described below:

JFR became 3:9
Job---------→ 3 months
Freedom--------→ 9 months

Currently my JFR looks like this:
Job (rat race) -------------→ 0%
Freedom to work on my dreams------→ 100%

Temporary employment Agencies

Let's be honest not everyone can jump out of the rat race cold turkey. We all must make a living somehow. Freedom can be achieved gradually and at one's own pace, depending on the need of each person. However, the best way for me was to step out of it as fast as I could. During the times that I was working a certain number of months out of the year, I signed up with a temporary employment agency. The beauty of these agencies is that they have assignments that can last from one day to several months. You give them your availability; tell them which assignments you prefer, and they will work with you. At my agency I chose the number of days I wanted to work, and for how long I wanted to work. I would only take assignments that I enjoyed doing. I find temporary employment agencies are a good option when you are weaning yourself out of the rat race. You too can reduce your Job vs Freedom ratio, and tailor it to your needs. However, you must cut your living expenses first, and stay focused.

Relocating you and your assets to a less expensive country

"Life is like riding a bicycle. To keep your balance, you must keep moving." **Albert Einstein**

America is not what it used to be. I remember the good old days when you could buy an apartment in NYC for less than 50,000 dollars and could rent a one bedroom apt for 600-800.Gone are those good days.

According to a Harvard study. Shockingly, almost 40 million Americans can't afford to pay for housing. The Joint center for housing states that home ownership in America has experienced a sharp decline. The housing market is increasing yet salaries are not. As a result, a lot of people who want to own are stuck renting due to the unaffordability of housing.

Barry Solomon a financial trend analyzer, is a Canadian expatriate, who now lives in the Caribbean. He states that in first world nations, currency values are deteriorating. Inflation is in full gear and the collapse of the US dollar is past the point of recovery. He predicts European nations are going toward a similar collapse. We can see this every day. When we notice that things are not as cheap as they use to be. Prices, even for consumer goods just keep going up. You can read more about Barry Solomon's predictions in his blog. Below is the address to his blog. http://www.drescapes.com/category/currency/

First world nations are very developed, they have a more robust economy and infrastructure. However, what is the catch 22? These nations can be expensive to live in and can make escaping the rat race a rather daunting task. However, what some people have done, and I include myself, they relocate themselves as well as their assets to less expensive countries. Often currencies such as the American dollar, euro, sterling pounds, stretch far in third world countries. The beauty of living in these third world countries is that your cost of living will decrease dramatically, and your quality of life could improve. For example, if you pay 2,000 dollars in rent to live in a shoebox apt in a big city in the USA. In a third world country, you can have a comfortable life with that amount. As an added perk, many of these nations. have lovely weather and breathtaking natural views. However, before you decide to sell your house, pack your things and go, there are some considerations you need to keep in mind. Below, I will be discussing some. I will also mention some countries where the cost of living is a lot less, thus making your escape from the rat race a lot easier.

Examples of countries with lower cost of living were people have relocated:
*Thailand
*Nicaragua
*Ecuador
*Dominican Republic
*Panama
*Malaysia
*Belize
*Mexico
*Colombia

To get an idea of what these countries' cost of living is, you can visit this website. http://www.numbeo.com/cost-of-living/comparison.jsp in this website, you enter the name of the city that you currently live in, and then you enter a city in your country of interest. The website will tell you how much you can expect to pay for things such as food, rent, clothes, utilities and more.

I Chose to relocate overseas. My home base is in the Dominican Republic. I now live in a less expensive country and this enabled me to get out of the rat race quicker. There are things that I considered before making this decision. I'm mentioning them Below:

Citizenship Requirements

It's important to know what the citizenship requirements are. Find out how you can get the country's citizenship card. It's very important as it allows you to do all kinds of transactions with in the country. Plus, you don't want to run into problems with immigration officials.

Cost of living

I analyzed the cost of renting a property vs buying. I also went to different neighborhoods and made comparisons. For me buying my house turned into a better option. Once it's paid off you live rent free. I also did my research asked people who owned homes, how much utilities could cost. I took a tour of local supermarkets and grocery stores to get a feel of how much food prices ran, as well as supplies and clothing. This help me to get a pretty clear picture of what the cost of living in this country could be.

Language

Relocating to a Spanish speaking country was no challenge for me because I speak Spanish fluently. However, if you decide to relocate to a country that does not speak your native tongue, consider learning the new language. You will have an easier time navigating your way through, as well as decreasing your chances of being scammed or ripped off.

Healthcare

You need to investigate healthcare options of this new land you are moving to. There is nothing more disheartening than getting sick in your new country and not having funds or insurance to help offset the cost of such catastrophic events. Investigate, what health insurance plans the new country has to offer. You need to know how much your cost will be, what the plan covers and when will the plan begin providing full coverage. Some health insurance plans have a grace period. Meaning that it can take up to six months for the full coverage to kick in. Once you spot a health insurance plan that you feel is right, it's not a bad idea to invest in one. Some expatriates wait out the insurance's grace period while still in their home country to avoid getting caught without health insurance.

Analyze the possibility of starting your own business overseas

Perhaps for some, starting your own business, is a good way to make a living in your new-found land. First, analyze what your passion is and turn it into a business. For me It is real estate, so I went that route. Before you dive into your business venture, get well informed about the business. Study the market, the cost, the opportunities, and laws of the land regarding business. Get information from people that are already successful in the business you want. Some business ideas overseas are: vacation rentals, real estate, setting up an English teaching school, bars, food business, working in location independent online businesses. Some decide to bring a new business idea into the new country. One expatriate for example decided to rent out transparent canoes at the beach and he is doing well in this business.

Investing in real estate overseas

If you sell your house in a first world nation, you can take the profit you made from the equity and invest it in rental properties in a different country. All the ideas of real estate investing that I discussed earlier can be applied overseas too. Depending on where you buy and how much equity you receive, your dollars or Euros can buy more properties in third world countries than in first world nations. Not only that but some countries have a lesser tax burden with real estate. You could live off your rental income overseas and kiss the rat race good bye forever.

The Job vs Freedom ratio concept overseas

Some expatriates rent or buy a property in a third world country where the rents are drastically, less expensive. Subsequently, they do freelance work for 6 months in their native first world nation, save their money, and then return for 6 months to the less expensive country to live on what they saved up. I have done this, and it has worked for me. It allowed me to invest even more and achieve more freedom. If you make a higher salary and you keep your expenses low, you could be working as little as 3-4 months and spend as much as 9 months in your new country. Where the living is easier, due to the cost of living being a fraction of the cost of first world nations.

Choosing a Location independent career

Ever been in a job you hate and wished for a career change? Before you take the leap of changing your career. Sit down and reflect. Don't ever take a career just because the money is good. It does not make any sense to put yourself through hard work for the money. Look into different career options and see if it's something you would enjoy doing. My advice, if you don't want to be stuck in the rat race, choose a career that is location independent. The beauty of these careers is that you can be sitting at the beach and working. All you will need is a laptop and an internet connection. You will not have to report to a specific address every day and spend 40 hours behind a cubicle every week. Your location would be up to you.

Web developer

Once you become a web developer, you can make this occupation mobile. All you will need is a laptop and an internet connection and you are ready to go. Web developers design and create websites They are responsible for the appearance of the site, as well as the sites' technical aspects. They monitor a website's performance and capacity. Also, they may create content for the site.

Requirements to become a web developer range from a high school diploma to a bachelor's degree. Web developers also need to have knowledge of both programing and graphic design. Below are a few sources online that give courses for free. You can take a tutorial and get a feel of what Web developers do and see if it is right for you before you spend money on a formal certificate course.

Resources for web developers

Job opportunity and tutorials:

https://upwork.com
http://www.learnlayout.com

Photographer

If you have a passion for photography, you can turn this into a business for yourself. There are companies online that will pay you for your great photos. You could earn royalty income, every time someone purchases and downloads your photo. Some companies pay a set amount for each sale of your photos. The company photo shelter allows you to make the sale through your own site. This in turn would enable you to earn more from the sales of your photos.

Online companies that to sell your photos

> http://www.alamy.com
> http://www.shutterstock.com
> http://www.istockphoto.com
> http://www.photoshelter.com

Graphic designer

Graphic designers take written or spoken ideas and convert them into designs, images and layouts. They can create these visual concepts with, computer software or by hand. Their art serves to inform, inspire and catch the eye of the consumers. On a day to day basis, we see the work of graphic designers being used in various applications such as advertisements, brochure and magazines.

To become a graphic designer, you will need a bachelor's degree. However; if you already have a bachelor's degree in another profession, you can pursue technical training in graphic design to meet most hiring requirements. On the next page, are some websites with tutorials in graphic design, so that you can get the feel of what graphic designers do.

Graphic design tutorial websites

http://www.alison.com
http://www.canva.com

Graphic Designer job opportunities:

https://www.99designs.com/designers
https://www.fiverr.com/start_selling

Translator

If you have the skill of speaking another language fluently, you can teach it online and not have to work 9-5. According to an article written by Ines Pimentel from the site digital donut, there are 10 languages that are at the top regarding business translation. The languages are written in the order of importance: 1) English 2) Chinese 3) Spanish 4) Arabic 5) German 6) Portuguese 7) Russian 8) French 9) Japanese 10) Hindi. Below are sites that offer online work for translators.

Websites for translator work opportunities

http://www.upwork.com/
http://www.translatorcafe.com
http://www.gengo.com
http://www.verbalizeit.com

If you already know any of the languages above, you can already be on to something. This skill could open other opportunities for you. Not only in being a translator but in having your own language lesson business. I will share a few examples of people who have prolific language blogs and sell their products too:

http://www.speakinglatino.com
httpwww.Mandarinhq.com

English teacher

English is a very important language globally. It is in demand and a lot of people want to learn it. People are willing to pay for English lessons. Below are sites that hire people who are interested in teaching English online. You can visit these sites and learn more about it.

http://www.vipkid.com
http://www.cambly.com
http://www.englishhunt.com
http://www.lingoda.com

Online consultant

If you have certifications and licenses in professions such as Marketing, accounting, computers, business, you can establish your own consulting business. Consultants conduct research to find out more about their client's company and needs. They develop strategies, new procedures and assess their pros and cons. Their game plan is to resolve problems for their clients. This business can become completely mobile and with proper research and preparation you can be your own boss. This link has information about flexible jobs in the consulting field: https://www.flexjobs.com/jobs

Homesteading

Homesteading can offer you an escape from the rat race. and if you mix this concept with other things such as real estate investing or with an online business this can be your ticket out of the rat race. The idea behind homesteading is that you choose to live a self-sustainable life. A life that is not dependent on the consumerism that exists in our society. This kind of lifestyle reduces your carbon foot print, and the earth will thank you too.

Owning a Homestead allows you to live mortgage and rent free. Homesteaders save money, buy a piece of land. Usually, this land is in the country and not inside big cities. they would buy an acre or two and build their own house, such as a log cabin. They create their own water wells and install solar panels for power. It's a lot of work in the beginning to set up but the rewards will be reaped later.

People that eliminate their largest expense, rent or mortgage and live off the land, reduce drastically, the need to have money. I have listed some popular homesteading blogs you can explore to get a better idea about this lifestyle and you can decide if it will be for you.

Homesteading blogs:

http://www.homesteadmania.com
http://www.thebackyardfarmingconnection.com
http://www.ouroneacrefarm.com

RV Life/ nomadic lifestyle
RV (recreational vehicle)

Are you adventurous? Want to try something really different? If you answered yes to both questions, then maybe a nomadic lifestyle and RV living can be for you.
RV life can offer a person the opportunities to get new and awe filled experiences. Instead of being assigned to a cubicle for 8 hours, you could travel around the country and experience the natural beauty and scenery, your country has to offer. All that without paying rent to a landlord! You can travel to several states or even who knows the 52 states? That would be up to you.

Nomadic lifestyle, where to begin?

1) Analyze how you are going to make a living on the road.

you have to have a plan of how you are going to make money while on the road traveling. You can travel as much as you want or as little as you want, depending on your budget. You don't have to be rich to have this lifestyle. As a nomad living in an RV, you can make a living in the following ways:

1.Job vs Freedom ratio concept. For example: work 6 months in a state with lots of job opportunities, save your money. Then you travel in your RV home for 6 months and live off your savings.

2.Real estate investment/Rental income (described above)

3. Location independent/online careers (described above)

4. If you have a skill such as mechanic, plumber, electrician, painter, handy man, you can order business cards and spread the word in the state you are at.

5. You can work in campgrounds. The links below, are websites that advertise jobs for nomads:
http://www.workampingjobs.com
http://www.happyvagabonds.com/jobs/jobs-by-state

2) Downsize
If you own a house or an apartment, and you own a lot of stuff, you have to analyze, how you are going to get rid of excess things. You can sell it or give it away. The decision is yours to make. Reason being, all your possessions must fit into your new RV home, which is a smaller space. If you click on the links below, you will be able to check out different types of RVs. You can also find bargains and deals on craigslist.

Types of RV http://www.rvusa.com/browse-all-rvs
To check out RV deals http://www.craiglist.org

3) Campground information

Campgrounds play an important part for people who live in the RV lifestyle. They are places where you can set up camp rest relax and enjoy the scenery. Also, they offer the opportunity to dump your RV's waste, replenish your water supply and recharge your batteries, to make your life more comfortable. Below are links that give you information about camp site throughout the United States:
http://www.reserveamerica.com
http://www.thousandtrails.com/membership-info

In conclusion, many people have taken the leap into the nomadic lifestyle. It offers lots of freedom, travel and adventure. Regular working people are doing it and so can you. Even people with children are embarking on this journey. Below I will be sharing a link of a blog that I have followed about a family that lives in an RV fulltime.

Fulltime RV family----→   https://winnebagolife.com

The formula to escape the rat race is up to you.

Inaction is the biggest killer of dreams and passion. If you want to get out of the rat race, but refuse to act on it, you are setting yourself for a life of drudgery and boredom. The formula to get out of the rat race can be different for everyone. There is no exact way. One person might combine different things that can produce an income. Some might do just one. Below are some examples:

Get out of the rat race plans

1. Real estate investment + relocation to less expensive country+ Location independent career.
2. Location independent career + RV lifestyle
3. Homesteading + Blogging + selling products on website
4. Job vs Freedom ratio concept + Short-term rentals
5. Selling your arts and crafts via your very own online store.

The list can go on about the different combination of things you can do, to get out of the rat race. The important thing is, that you have to shape your scape plan to suit your particular needs.

Chapter 10.

Life is only one, make the best out of it.

The regrets of the dying

There is an adage that says: 'death and taxes are the only guarantees that one has in life.' That statement couldn't be truer. Many people have not woken up and smelled the roses yet about life and death. We only get one life. Therefore, we should try to live it as best as we can.

Bronnie Ware, a nurse working with people in their death bed, decided to poll dying patients, asking them what they most regretted in life. She realized there were 5 things people regretted the most. However, I will be sharing 3 of her findings as well as my own interpretations of them. They are as follows:

"I wish I had the courage to live a life true to myself, not the life others expected of me."

"Fear is a rope that pulls you away from what you really want to do. Cut the rope today!" **Indiana Quezada**

Most people in society approve conventional life choices. Get a job, marry, buy a house, have children, retire at after 60. Unconventional life choices are often frowned upon. Therefore, many don't do what they really want to do, out of fear of what people will think of them. In other words, they spend their lives being crowd pleasers If you are always trying to please other people, you will not be able to live your life. Instead live a life true to yourself.

"I wish I hadn't worked so hard."

The cost of living in the USA is at an all-time high. Many Americans cannot afford to buy a house and are stuck renting. If they manage to own a home, they sometimes must have more than one job, to be able to pay the bills. Count in the cost of having kids. In some cities the care for 1 child is about $1000 dollars a month. Some people pay more than that. All these high cost of living expenses make people spend a lifetime working very hard for money. As a result, at the end of life, it becomes a regret.

"I wish I had let myself be happy."

"In twenty years, you'll regret the things you didn't do rather than the things you did do." **Mark Twain**

What this tells us is that happiness is a choice. Our life choices can make or break us when it comes to happiness. It is up to us if we are going to have a vacation, travel, have a family, kids. We have the power to embrace things that makes us happy and staying that way.

From the above 3 regrets of the dying, we can learn a very valuable lesson. Are you noticing the pattern here? They are regretting not doing the things that they really wanted to do. Now is the time to act and do the things that we really want to do and make ourselves happier! Otherwise, Years down the line, we will end up regretting what we didn't do.

Unfortunately, the human life span is too short. According to Wikipedia, human life expectancy in the USA is 79 years. If you are lucky, you can get to live a little more. This means that by the time we hit our forty's, we have already lived half of our lifetime, if not less. Even though we have a limited time on earth, many people continue to choose staying in unhappy situations.

Since we have a limited time on earth, and perhaps illnesses could set in our older years, why not do something different and enjoy the heck out of your life, while you are still young and have the energy to do so? Why keep putting it off for tomorrow, when tomorrow is not guaranteed?

Waking up and smelling the roses

After I woke up and smelled the roses about life, I made some lifestyle changes. I used to work full time jobs. Nowadays, I work on my own terms. I choose the amount of time that I will be working. This is the happiest I have ever been, and I am not rich.

After making this life change, I have freed up more time to spend with my family. I take more vacations. I have been to several islands in the Caribbean, several countries in Europe, I've taken road trips across different states in the USA. In my travels, I have enjoyed awesome views in nature. One time when I was arriving to the USA from overseas, the immigration officer that stamped my passport noticed all the stamps in my passport and said: "How do you manage take so many vacations?" Most people can't travel like that. I couldn't travel like you."
Freedom is very important to me. It makes me happy. I was able to achieve it by being committed to freeing

myself. The path out of the rat race is not easy, but it is possible to get out.

Life is nothing but a short journey. It can be here today, gone by tomorrow. I would rather be like a shooting star full of energy and light, positively charged and not a bunch of fallen leaves lying motionless, in their own decay.
If you were stranded in an island and a life boat came by, would do anything in you power to attract its attention, to be rescued? or would you lay motionless in the sand and risk perishing? Are you going to live your life? or are you going to just exist? Ultimately, the decision is up to you. Life can be like a ship and you are its captain. You decide what direction it will head.

The End

WORKS CITED

https://www.cnbc.com/2017/07/13/harvard-study-heres-how-many-americans-cant-afford-housing.html

https://www.fool.com/retirement/2018/06/15/fact-or-fiction-social-security-is-running-out-of.aspx

https://bronnieware.com/blog/regrets-of-the-dying/

https://www.digitaldoughnut.com/articles/2017/february/the-top-10-languages-in-higher-demand-for-business

ABOUT THE AUTHOR

Indiana Quezada is an up and coming author. Her home base is in the Dominican Republic. She writes about her passions. 9 to 5 until 65 is ridiculous, is her first book. Indiana loves to inform and inspire people.

By the way…...

If you found this book, helpful and inspirational. Please give me a review. Your support is very important to me and is very much appreciated. Thank you in advance for your support.

Thank you again for supporting me!

www.ingramcontent.com/pod-product-compliance
Lightning Source LLC
Chambersburg PA
CBHW021501210526
45463CB00002B/844